Relationship Success Tips: Tips for a Healthy, Loving, Well-Connected Relationship

Simple everyday ways to succeed in your relationship, beginning right now.

BARBARA ANN WILLIAMS

Relationship Success Tips: Tips for a Healthy, Loving, Well-Connected Relationship

Barbara Ann Williams

© 2016, 2018 by Barbara Ann Williams

All rights reserved. This book was self-published by the author Barbara Ann Williams. No part of this book may be reproduced in any form by any means without prior written permission of the author. This includes reprints, excerpts, photocopy, electronic, recording, or any future means of reproducing text.

ISBN-13: 978-1719062282
ISBN-10: 1719062285

Designed and edited by Julia T Williams

For any of the aforementioned acts, please contact Barbara Ann Williams at https://barbaraannwilliams.com.

Published in the United States.

Introduction

The idea for this book came from a compilation of relationship tips I wrote in my monthly newsletter, Heart Connections. It's where I offered tips, ideas, suggestions, recommendations, personal thoughts, and ways individuals and couples could improve their relationships.

It was such fun for me to come up with these as I would write regularly, even in my weekly blogs; not to mention the questions that would come up, which continued to inspire more ideas.

My recommendation for you as you go through this quick and easy read is to just go straight through it without stopping or giving it too much thought while reading. Let it marinate in your mind, then later return with the intention of making notes along the way of what you can use to create success in your relationship, from wherever it is right now.

Ultimately, this is my wish for you: to come away with tips for having a successful relationship. The tough part is to take the tips and use them. They can be used in many ways, so be creative with what works best for you. Some ideas could be:

- Group discussions with other individuals or couples
- Individually read one tip and then discuss or share thoughts
- Use as a personal journal and reflect on a tip each day
- Hang post-it notes when something strikes a cord

Now begin your journey and come up with your own after your first read.

Enjoy!

3 THINGS THAT GREATLY AFFECT & INFLUENCE YOUR RELATIONSHIP:

1

Your thoughts.

2

Your feelings.

3

Your behavior.

Your thinking—whether positive or negative—will affect and influence your behavior and your relationships with the same results: positive or negative.

THOUGHTS AFFECT FEELINGS.

The way you think affects the way you feel, and the way you feel is tied into your actions and behaviors.

> JUST ABOUT EVERYTHING YOU DO IS A DIRECT RESULT OF THE WAY YOU FEEL.

Thoughts.

They affect your relationships greatly.

If you're not feeling okay, check what you're thinking about and how it's influencing everything else; especially your relationship.

Change the thought and you automatically change the feeling.

Change the feeling and you most definitely influence what you do and how you behave.

A COMMITTED RELATIONSHIP IS A PARTNERSHIP.

*A committed relationship is a partnership; it is not about finding the right person, but more about **being** the right person. So **be** what it is you want in someone else.*

Demonstrate for yourself that what you want is indeed possible in someone else.

MAKE MORE DEPOSITS THAN WITHDRAWALS.

*Make more deposits **into** your relationship than you do withdrawals **from** it.*

Invest where you want a return.

> **WHAT YOU CAN'T SELL AT HOME, DON'T TRY TO EXPORT ELSEWHERE.**

While a daily dose of communication may connect and breed intimacy, be sure to watch the timing of what you communicate.

Timing is key.

LISTENING REQUIRES FOCUSED ATTENTION.

Listening requires focused attention on what the other person is saying, and not thinking of what you plan to say when they're done.

Being right should not make your partner feel like a loser.

Go for a win-win.

> **TRY ATTRACTING INSTEAD OF ATTACKING.**

Communication is more than just talking.

If the person you're speaking to does not understand you, you're speaking into the air and wasting words. How much sense does that make?

*Make what you say pull the person in closer **to** you; not push further away **from** you.*

Be mindful that the way you treat your mate reflects what is going on inside you.

So, pay attention to what's going on within.

Take inventory of your own "stuff."

Notice your mood and where it's coming from, rather than spreading more of the same.

If you're not aware of your own "stuff", and put it in check, it's going to bleed over into your relationship in some way.

PAY ATTENTION TO THE SEEDS YOU SOW.

The thoughts you entertain will be planted as seeds to grow and come back stronger.

> "WHATSOEVER THINGS ARE TRUE...THINK ON THESE THINGS."

"Whatsoever things are true, whatsoever things are honest, whatsoever things are just, whatsoever things are pure, whatsoever things are lovely, whatsoever things are of good report; if there be any virtue, and if there be any praise, think on these things."

Philippians 4:8, KJV

> HAVE A PICTURE IN MIND OF WHAT YOU WANT.

Success is about striving for something you want to have or experience in your life, and then achieving it.

It's no different in your relationship, if you want it to be a success.

You have to be willing to put in the time, effort, energy and work needed to make sure it's what you want.

That means you need a picture in mind of what you want for yourself and your life.

Until you have that picture, you won't know what to create.

Be clear that you will always be creating something, consciously or unconsciously.

Make what you create intentional; knowing in the outset it's what you want.

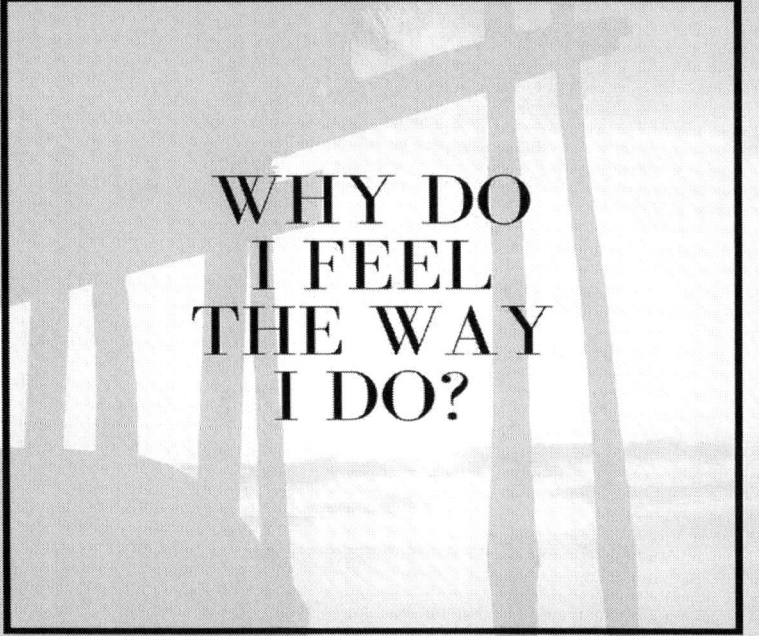

Take some time to do some inner reflecting to see what you come up with.

Look through some magazines and take out the time to feel what jumps out at you and ask yourself, "Why do I feel the way I do?"

If you don't know this, you can't expect for someone else to.

You are the one to help others understand you; so, take the time to "get" you.

WHAT'S YOUR DESIRED DESTINATION?

To move from where you are you must have some idea of where you want to be, or else you'll never move.

And if you do move without a desired destination in mind, you'll find the same discontentment in that movement.

There is little hope of success for the relationship that does not have a central purpose or definite goal at which to aim.

What's yours?

Living without a purpose is like driving without a destination.

You can live until you just die, which is to drive until you give out of gas.

But where would you be going until that happens?

You're more apt to succeed if you do what comes naturally, which is already instilled within you.

Let that drive you and your relationship to success.

LOOK FOR WHAT YOU WANT MORE OF.

Look for the feelings you want more of and create an environment that embraces them.

Set the stage for the life and relationship you want.

It is up to you.

IGNITE THE PASSION IN YOUR RELATIONSHIP.

Remember how you first met and see if there's something there to rekindle now.

Look for current and mutual attractions (mental, emotional, physical, spiritual, etc.) to help you rekindle the flame.

COMPLIMENT OFTEN.

Make dates and compliments a part of your regular routine.

Be present for one another.

REFLECT ON WHERE YOU ARE RIGHT NOW.

Take a moment to reflect on your life from where you are right now.

Not just the place, but more specifically, the position and the feel of it.

Are you happy and at peace right now where you are?

If you are, great!

But if you're not, guess what, you are the ONLY one who can change that; the only one.

Stop and look at your situation and decide what it is you want for yourself and your life and create steps to get you there.

Begin with step one: Act.

Step two...

Change just one thing in your life or relationship and see how it changes other things.

What do you think about it?

How do you feel about it?

What else changed as a result?

Make a new friendship or get rid of one that's draining you of creative energy.

Be mindful that this new friend will in some way reflect and/or represent you.

So, allow it to be a picture in your mind of how the world sees you.

This will affect you and other relationships.

The purpose is to see where you are.

It's a check point.

Open up and be willing to try something new and different.

Be about some type of growth, beginning from a personal space.

DON'T WAIT UNTIL YOU ARE EMPTY.

Don't wait until you have invested an enormous amount of your time, effort, energy, money, and most importantly, yourself, into a relationship before deciding it's not what you really want.

Be honest with yourself.

Don't tolerate what you're not willing to live with long-term, just for the sake of saying you're in a relationship.

QUALIFY THE INVESTMENT.

Determine your requirements, needs, and wants for a relationship, and qualify the investment before you're too far in.

As long as the problem is given fuel, it will remain in your life.

Focusing on the problem causes it to stay.

Nurture what you want to grow because your relationship will be as successful as your thoughts are about it.

Make them productive, joyful, and healthy.

ENCOURAGE HEALTHY RELATIONSHIPS.

Loving yourself will show others how to treat you by the way you do first.

Smile, be kind, open and friendly—it's attractive and draws others.

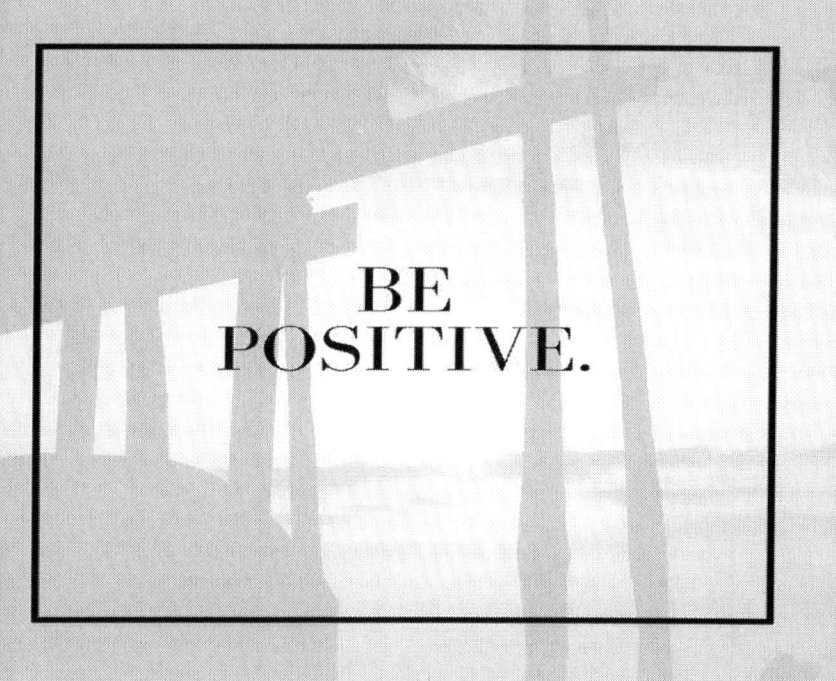

Be positive and willing to listen as much as, or more than you talk; you'll learn a lot faster about the other person.

KEEP YOUR RELATIONSHIP ALIVE.

Notice when things are becoming boring, stale, and repetitious, then make some changes.

*Strengthen your desire to have a better life,
then set a plan in place to bring it to pass.*

Go out on a date, and slowly add a little romance to get you back into the swing of connecting.

You define what romance looks like and how it feels for you.

Don't yell or raise your voice at one another unless the house is on fire, or it's a matter of life and death.

Create and develop what you want to feel around each other.

This is your responsibility.

Set the stage.

Be the first to speak and say a kind word when there's tension in the air.

Don't wait on the other person to make the first move.

Be the big, bold, loving individual you are and welcome your partner to reciprocate.

Look for reasons to have a little mercy and be a little more forgiving; they will come in handy when you need them.

Show and give what you want to be shown and given.

Don't beat yourself up or be too hard on yourself when a relationship has ended.

Be gentle.

Take time to mourn the loss, then brush yourself off, and set new goals for your future while embracing lessons learned.

Seek closure before moving forward.

Bid farewell.

Think about what it is you want for your life and be careful not to settle for anything less than that.

MAKE REVISIONS WHERE NEEDED.

Revise your requirements: What do you consider deal breakers?

Revise your needs: What do you really want?

Negotiate or renegotiate the update.

Clarify your wants and preferences in your relationship.

Don't back down.

When you take out the time to be loving and caring toward yourself, it's not difficult at all to share the same with others.

What can you do to show those positive loving-characteristic traits that we are all so in need of?

You can start by:

- *Looking a passerby in the eyes and saying hello*

- *Smiling at someone*

- *Holding the door open for someone*

- *Saying thank you*

If these don't build your relationship, they will most certainly help you feel good about you.

Find a full length mirror and give yourself a really good look over.

What do you see?

How do you feel about what you see?

What do you like about what you see?

What would you like to change about what you see?

Now step away from all the judgment and criticism of yourself and tell the person in the mirror, "You're okay."

How does that feel?

SETTLE
IT
WITHIN
YOURSELF.

Relieve yourself from all the pressures of trying to change in an instant the reflection in the mirror.

Settle it within yourself that you really are okay right now just as you are.

Period!

That acceptance will go a long way in your other relationships.

As the saying goes, in order for you to go where you have never gone before, you must be willing to do something you have never done.

The key here is willing.

Set your intention on taking action NOW.

Start off "right" and then go into maintenance mode.

You can do this!

> **BE CAREFUL NOT TO BE TOO QUICK AT LOOKING OUTWARD.**

If you're not enjoying the life you are experiencing, be careful not to be too quick at looking outward and blaming others.

First take a close look inside and see what's going on internally, because it is somehow a reflection of what's going on there.

Once you make some much needed changes internally, it will be reflected in the relationship in some way.

To get clear on anything, you must be willing to let go of everything that's not already clear.

If you let go of anything that is to be a part of you, don't worry over letting it go; it will somehow manage to show up again.

Trust that!

Decide*—just make a decision and move forward; only then will you know if that's what you want or not.*

Take action*—on what you decide.*

Evaluate*—and determine what to do next as a result of your outcome.*

Whatever you believe about yourself to be true, is.

It's about your own beliefs.

You make them so; or not.

OWN YOUR THOUGHTS, FEELINGS, & BEHAVIOR.

What you see, think, feel, believe, and experience belongs only to you.

*What you **choose** to see, think, feel, believe, and experience **about** this, also belongs **only** to you.*

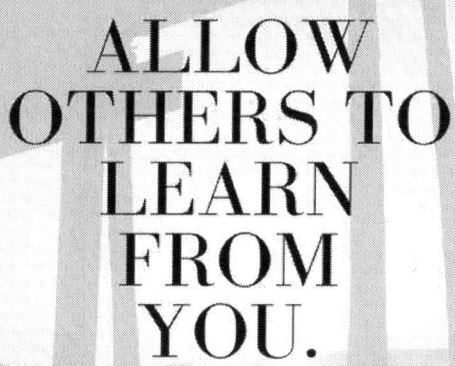

Remember this when it comes to dealing with others:

Not everyone sees, thinks, feels, believes, or experience things exactly as you do.

Allow them to learn from you, while you're open to learn from them.

This is what makes a relationship, a relationship.

Just because you feel like you've lost that loving feeling doesn't mean you can't get it back.

If you truly do want it, then begin to feed and nurture what you wish to receive in your life and in your relationship, and watch it grow.

If you're struggling in your relationship, it might not be such a bad idea to stop and reflect on where you stand—personally—in the relationship.

It will give you some insight into what you may need to look at a little more closely.

I want to express my sincere appreciation and thanks to Julia Blues, with The Storyprint, for her dedication in helping me see this publication to fruition. We went back and forth untiring through the grueling process of reading, writing, editing, sizing, and on and on and on. Thank you, Toot!

To my husband, Gary, who swooped me from under my mom's apron strings at such a tender young age and took me away in matrimony. It has been through this union that I have grown through the myriad of experiences that courtship, commitment, and growth in our marriage contributed to this work of art called writing.

To my parents, Jewell and Joe Griffin (both deceased), who were my first models of a real relationship.

To Gary Jr. and Julia, the two adults born to this union; you have added to the triumph of these tips, and in my ability to maintain a relationship with your father while raising you, and through observing you in your own relationships.

To those who have spent any time talking to and listening with me about all the many ideas I had going on in my head at any given time—my siblings, Gail, Jeannie, Sharon, and Neil; and especially to you, Miriam (one name and person I can never forget).

And to the many untold names of faces I've seen, talked to, and worked with over the decades through my practice as a professional. Thank you for how you and your stories and our times together has helped me in creating writings (newsletters, articles, blogs, anthologies, and poems) that helped both you and me through challenging times.

To each of you, I say THANKS! I am forever grateful.

Barbara

Now that you have gone through and finished *Relationship Success Tips*, you can come up with different ideas to support your relationship in new ways. Because of the size of this book, it is easy for you to go back through it again and again and gain even more insights. As you go through it the next time, stop and take the time to highlight, underline, and make physical and mental notes of ideas that can propel you forward.

I trust this has been very helpful to and for you. Grab a copy for an acquaintance, friend or loved one you know will be a blessing to as well.

Reach out and connect if you have questions, would like to take it a step further, or to receive personal relationship coaching help.

Visit BarbaraAnnWilliams.com for more information.

Barbara Ann and husband, Gary Williams, of 43 years and counting.

Thanks for reading!

Made in the USA
Columbia, SC
04 September 2018